I will wait for you

LOIS WYSE

American Greetings Corporation
Cleveland, Ohio 44144

Published by American Greetings, American Road, Cleveland, Ohio 44144.
First printing, June, 1971. Copyright, 1971, by Lois Wyse.
Library of Congress Catalogue Card Number: 79-157559
Printed in the United States of America
An American Greetings Book

I have.
I do.
I will.

I Will Wait for You

Remember that day you
Stood outside the restaurant in New York?
You were at one door,
I was at another,
And so we waited . . .
Lost to each other . . .
We never knew
We were close enough to touch
Until you came around the corner.

There have been other corners in
Our wildly mixed-up lives,
Yet I have stood
In sun and sickness
I have waited 'til you picked the time
To round the corner
And smooth the roughest part of life:
The waiting time.

So, my love,
At this moment
Even though you stand alone
You can be sure
That any time you turn the corner
You will find me there.

I will wait for you.

If Someone Else Answers, I'll Hang Up

Alone is satisfactory
When I know
You are also
Alone.

      You are alone,
      Aren't you?

I Do More Than Clean Drawers When You Are Away

Do not despair
Of days we do not share,
For well-spent solitude
Can strengthen
The delicate nerve-endings of love.

Where Are You?

It is thundering, and I am alone.
In this rumbling silence
I can hear
What happens to a lot of frightened people.
I am one of them.

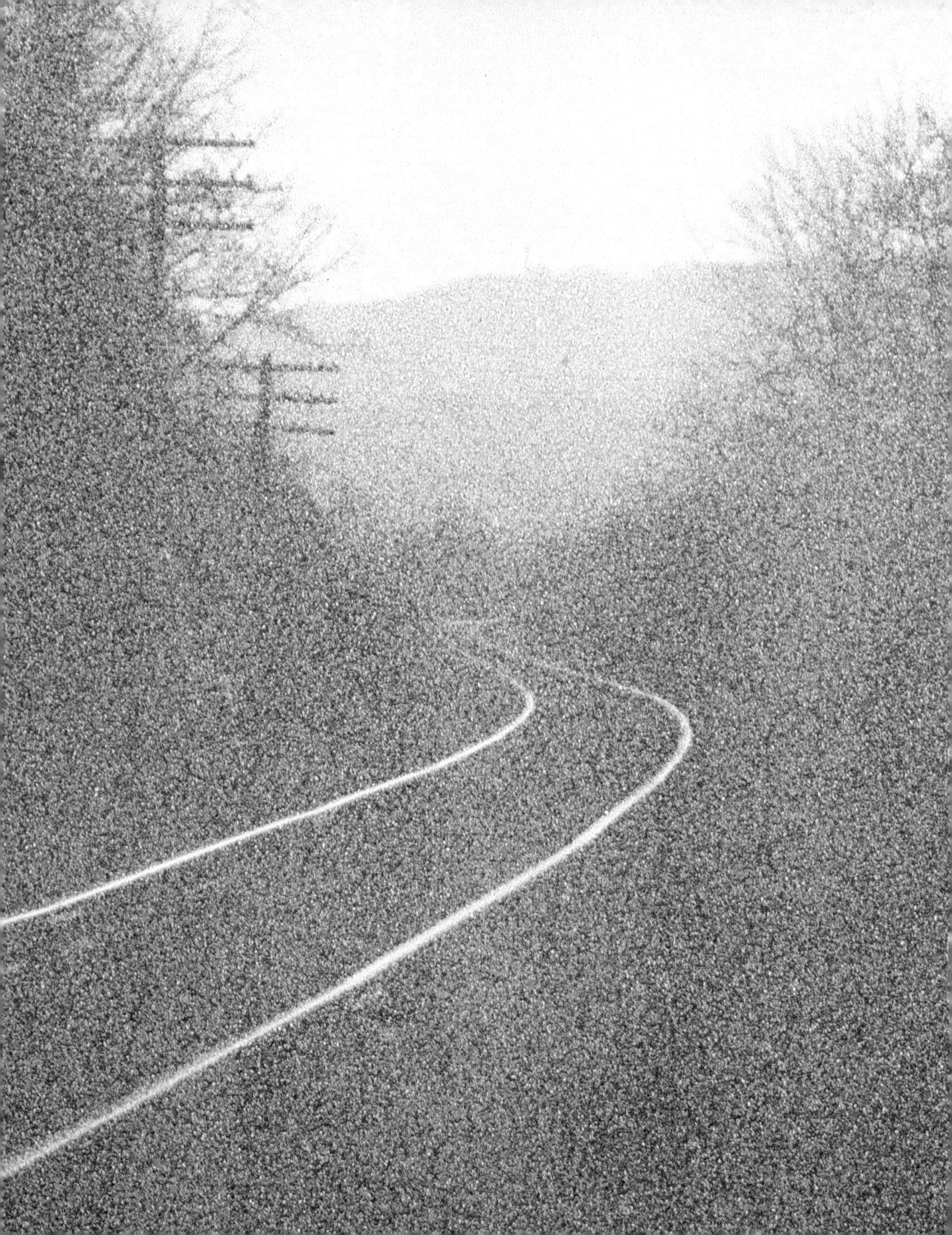

Geography for Lovers

Love has
A longitude and latitude
All its own.
So please don't go away again,
For when you do
You change
The degree of love
Between you and me.

Out of Sighs

My sighs are
The measure of my missing you.
This is an eight-sigh day.
An improvement.
For I have also had
My eight-day sighs.

Still I Wait for You

While I wait for you,
I do not review
This day or any other.

In my mind I seek
A painting by Chagall,
Some lines of Dickinson,

And, wonder of wonders,
Framed between lines
I find you.

The Waiting Game

We are not the same, are we, dear?
I mean a year ago I didn't know what lay ahead
And I guess it was good that I didn't
Because maybe I really couldn't have stood it at all.

But now it is past.

I feel the fresh wind of tomorrow,
And I am glad this year is over,
And I am glad you love me so much,
But I wish it hadn't taken a year like this to prove it.

Solitude

In solitude
We reinforce the decisions
Made together.

No Simple Test

Separation is not a simple test of love.
It is a test of sanity.
Can I function apart from you?
Can you think away from me?

When Do You Love Me?

Do not encrust me
With golden virtue
I never can possess,
For if you do
You will, in time,
Love me most
When we are apart.

All of Life is Not Resolved

The lights are trained on me.
I bask and burn in the brightness of it all,
Yet, somehow, despite the glare
I still work in darkness.
      Brighter lights, please.
      Stronger lights next.
I still can't see the answers.

The Author

Lois Wyse is the author of best-selling books of
love poetry, including "Love Poems For The Very Married",
"Are You Sure You Love Me?", and "I Love You Better Now",
as well as the popular non-fiction book, "Mrs. Success".
Her articles and poems appear regularly in numerous
magazines in the United States and abroad.

Lois Wyse, her husband Marc, and their two children,
Katherine and Robert, live in Shaker Heights, Ohio.